Born Behind Bars

By. Mitchell Paschall Jr.

Dedication

I would like to dedicate this book to my greatest inspiration, the youth in my hometown, Baltimore Maryland. I wish for this to be a form of hope and inspiration. That these words will reach someone if not many and fuel persistence and endurance. I love you.

Secondly, I'd like to thank my grandparents who raised me in an environment that allowed me to explore my creativity and nurture the strong, wise and patient man that I am. Lillie Paschall, you are more than a grandmother to me, you are my soul sister! You are one being I know for damn sure I chose this life to see again! I love you.

Last but not least, my mother Valerie Chandler. There is no other experience, person or accomplishment that can match what I was gifted with in having you as a mother. Mom, to date you are the strongest person I've ever met. You are the most loving, sacrificial, bravest, encouraging and down to earth soul that walked this earth. Thank you for the gifts that keep on giving. I love you.

Introduction

All my life I've dealt with depression. At times the only release or momentarily escape was through writing. My prison was my state of mind and lack of faith which constantly altered my perception of reality. As early as seven, I felt consumed by violence, abandonment, being misunderstood and unaccepted. It wasn't until I got older that I experienced the epiphanies that lead me to self realization and salvation. I then began to take a closer look at the world, which led me on the path of studying the "Systems" that we are all affected by, or forced to be subjected to. What I discovered motivated me to escape and inspire others as well.

I didn't realize I had a book inside of me that was pretty much already written, until 2014. It was during this time I'd begin really questioning my purpose in life. Through prayer and meditation, I discovered that I'd been writing far longer than I'd been doing anything else in life. Before barbering, before acting, before football, I was a writer. I then started revisiting poems, essays and random creative writings dating back from middle school, and to my astonishment, I saw my own growth. A lot of it I couldn't believe I wrote. Most of my writing has no titles because I rarely began writing with any specific intention. By the grace of God, oftentimes I'm just able to scribe my emotions and collective experiences. I then realized that these words weren't just for me. That they were delivered to me to share. This book is intended to encourage and liberate as well as share my passion for music and rhythmic vernacular. The title "Born Behind Bars" is a play on words. The first meaning addresses the feeling of being born into oppression either it be from society, circumstance, or state of mind. The second addresses the poetry and music that has existed inside of me since a child. Through expression, I found liberation. Getting it out - got me out.

Sleeping to sounds of sirens.
Dreams lasting through sounds of gunshots blasting.
Little kids playing knick or knock.
Bored from having to sit and watch.
Or from toting rocks in their socks.
So the doe boys can work the blocks,
For those who want to come and cop.
Day in day out, 24/7 nonstop.
Living off nothing more than a half
and half and chicken box.

Hope is gained after the age of twenty-five.
For faith lies in those who escape their fate.

Breeding is both bold and brave.
So all offspring innately go hard from the cradle to the grave.

Like a broken compass, most live with no direction.
Many are contracting due to unthoughtful actions.
For here it is best to stay strapped up and wrapped up twice
for protection.

Overnight changing from the city that reads to the city that bleeds.

From Baltimore to body more.
A City where most would ignore a tour.
Or detour before ever driving through the streets of B-more.

Beauty lies underneath true lies of those who view with
blinded eyes

A muted television with no captions.
Talents with no actions.
White and black tees become fashion.

Believe they say,
A picture of the future has yet to change.
What I saw still remains.
Because the same picture still lies in the same frame.
Same game, different state but relevant aim.
Causing the same pains.
Leaving the same stains.
My brothers killing brothers, no different
then the slaying of Abel by Cain.
I pray my fame will bring sustain.

The Revolution should be televised, everything else is
Great deeds should be recognized.
But instead we repeatedly see who gets shot and who dies.

Out our mouths we cry, and through our eyes we speak.

Land of the unfree but home of the brave.
Systematic chains keep the ignorant enslaved.

Now big brothers watching.
State profiting off pick pocketing.
From money made through vowel and bag cropping.

Plot thickens.
Pharmacy administering poison.
Tossed burners become toys and
With no reasoning.
Constant pain through all seasons.

And let me not forget to mention.
Instead of schools, more juvenile detentions.
Dumb down education.
More like mental lynching.
Since when did we start hiring scholastic henchmen.

Survival of the fit.
SIKE, survival of the rich.

Kissed with hard life, hugged with misfortunes.
Our youths' wishes are dismissed, their needs erased from the list.
The only joy found is through lit bliss or a few sips of
misconceptions.

Hold me not accountable for my words.
Sound expressions.
But let my tone not be your deception.
Just feelings that slept thin.
Then awakened when fear of no resolution crept in.

So because, for every cause there's an effect.
I shall not pause or not let my city fall to neglect.

I tried to save all of them all because of you

All because of you I couldn't love them like I loved you

Never witness a man love you like I do

They never worshipped you

They had no honor for you

They only wanted to bring harm to you

So women came to me without even a clue

That my eager love stems from the lack of love they all showed them and you

I set my goals in something unattainable

Like how could I believe that true love could conquer all

All of them

Like each and everyone

Or all that they were

Acting like God and miraculously reconstructing a broken heart

Broken mind or even better a broken spirit

Let alone trying to resurrect my own

Trying to talk to someone with two broken cellular phones

That's how signals get crossed

That's how feelings get tossed

Bridging the gap of generations cursed by neglect

I soon found out what would become the cost

I first discover this in 7th grade English with my teacher
miss moss

She push me to find me

Every weekend journal entry became time to define me

She grabbed my mind and found me, the real me,
that I am, that I was or could be

So blame her for the constant over analyzing

Yet thank her for planting the seeds that planted seeds

That healing from systematic or genetic depression could be achieved

Encouraging you to be bold and wear your heart on ya sleeve

That there's nothing wrong with using love as a defense or weapon

That the fact that I'm like no one else is what makes me special

And yet each day you wrestle with identity and status quo

Wrestle with seeing all women as Queens even the so call, well you know

Fighting to prove your manhood, in a hood with no men

With your hood off, being unnatural trying not to grin
One slight sign of comfort would make someone check ya chin.

No fathers around, so women have to behave like men.
Little boys have to be harder than hard, cause girls are being groomed to be like them
In a game where nobody wins.

So I fight in life, enduring every loss.

Trying not to become numb and lose myself in the struggle.

I mean I'm a lover and fighter.

But I love her too much to fight her.

Momma ain't raise no punk.

The blocks I grew on ain't take no chumps.
No victory is won without some bruises and bumps.

You choose to get stumped then you choose to get stomped.

She gave me life, she gave her life.

That's why I call her my Messiah.

All that she endured gave me strength to endure and even
help me detour from that which she endured.

That's why I call you my Momma comma Queen comma
Goddess comma Strong comma Beautiful comma
You comma You comma You and You.

My Queens, my struggles, my dreams.

You owe me nothing and no one can take advantage of
what's given free.

I had dreams once, young man.
I once was courageous.
All that I wanted to be, was just as far as I could reach.
I entered my dreams and lived there for quite some time.
Yes young man, I was unstoppable,
invincible, indestructible,
And life was a stream.
I once had dreams.
Now it all seems.
Like a poorly plotted scheme.
Or like dull dry hair covered with sheen.
Young man I constantly wake up to reality's reality.
Brutally faced with my current totality.
Inadvertently and suddenly I stopped reaching.
Haunted by who I was and running from who I've become.
Only the days move me forward, all else remains stuck.
Stuck between how great I was and how great I
know I can be, it all seems preposterous.
A reformed optimus turned pessimist.
The place I feel most comfortable.
If one lives in defeat, then all future defeats are purely
one's embraced life.
A comfortably placed knife.
In the gut.
Never budging.
A feasible pain.
A feasible slain.

See I look back at you and I see what was once me.
Praying that in the future we both only
look forward, toward our best self.
Young man I once viewed the world at my feet instead of
my shoulders.
That was before you became me.
And I got older.

I had dreams once young man
I once was courageous
All that I wanted to be, was just
as far as I could reach
I entered my dreams and lived there
for quite some time
Yes young man, I was unstoppable
invincible indestructible
And life was a stream
I once had dreams
Now it all seems
Like an pooly plotted scheme
Or like dull dry hair covered
with sheen
Young man I constanly wake up
to reality's reality,
Brutally faced with my current
totality,
Inadvertenly and suddehnly I
stopped reaching
Haunted by who I was and
running from who I've become
Only the days move me forward
all else remains stuck
Stuck behind how great I was and how
great to know I can be) it all seems preposterous

A reformed Optimus turned
pessimist
If one lives in defeat, than all
future failures are purely ones
embranced life
A comfortably placed knife
In the gut
Never bridging
A feasible pain
A feasible slain
See I look back at you and I
see what was once me
Praying that in the future we
both only look forward, toward
our best self
Young man I once viewed the
world at my feet instead of my
shoulders
That was before you became me
And I got older

It's been a minute since I vented.
Words as my prescription and the net as my clinic.
This space in time I know now is rented.
It'll come and go in an instant.
So I choose now, with nouns and vowel sounds.
Like loose bowels and that's so splendid.
I gave my all to everyone and everything,
leaving nothing behind.
Inclined to rewind that which was spent, but instead
I'm left rinsed, purged of my past life karma,
Never meaning to harm them,
But armed with bars from a far,
With a hug and a grin, but yes I admit I sin.
I'm a sinner, I'm a winner, I'm like hot coals in the winter.
Souls old, been told since a tenor.
Now my notes are baritone, so deep I'm left alone, a cold stone.
Nothing Splenda, I'm as naked as can be, far from a pretender.

Since I was a boy, five years old, my life has been filled with trauma. In fact, I got in the habit of being over analytical out of just protection, defense to prepare for the unexpected. Calculating every move so I wouldn't get hurt. My mother fell victim to drugs heavy around six or seven and that's when I had to transform into a man from a boy. I had to protect her and my sister. I'd wake up in the middle of the night, sneak in her purse, dump out the residue dope and hide her pipes. Jumping in between fights when men were trying to beat her up.

By nine or ten she would start abandoning us for hours or what seemed like whole days. Sometimes we would take turns sleeping at night, out of fear and anticipation for my mother's arrival. I mean we loved her **SO MUCH** that we would fight over who would sleep in the middle, because we both wanted to sleep next to her.

At such a young age, I couldn't handle the person I looked up to with the highest regard, exploring their sexuality with men other than my step father. Looking in her eyes after her face was swollen from a nigga beating the shit out of her. Looking in her eyes at eleven or twelve asking her if she was high and her lying to me. All that pain sitting on my heart, should have made me abusive to women, never trusting them, killing their spirit and bodies. But instead I chose to have empathy and love them the way my mother should have been loved. And I got played by them all, cause they all turned out to be just as manipulative, somewhat reckless as her and hurt; thus hurting me.

So I cry because I have pain, and I can't store it in anymore. I just want to love and be loved. I want loyalty, **HONESTY** and integrity. I laughed at your mom on the inside when she said men don't give up, cause I've been fighting not giving up since I was nine years old. Through all of this, I had no father involved, no one to validate my efforts, or to celebrate my accomplishments. I felt totally unwanted, my two biological parents didn't want me. Thus causing me to create a false external confidence just to get by, and not be attacked.

My strength is my heart, my love for love, my ability to forgive, and my endurance. I'm very intuitive and I have mastered recognising the faces of liars and manipulators all my life. I know when someone isn't being a hundred. Last night you were forcing yourself to be cool. You didn't touch me, returned no affection, you complained about my daughter for **EVERY** move she made and then later, as soon as there was an opportunity to end it, you took it. Then tried to downplay it all.

I cried because I loved you, but I don't think you'll ever be totally comfortable with being open and honest as I need you to be. And that's a harsh reality. Plus on top of all this, I have to work on me, us, and being a father to my kids whose moms can be extremely difficult. It's a lot. Always has been, but I'm still here, working at it.

I don't expect anyone to take on my burdens, but just love me and be naked with me. Totally transparent with me, so that can be at least one thing I don't have to question, in a life where I've been conditioned to question **EVERYTHING**.

I'm in the dark.
Lights are out.
The energy bill got too expensive.
So we lost connections.
In an abandoned building structured for two.
Solitude is less expensive.
No reception through these walls either.
Signals lost.
Second party couldn't pay the cost.
So I'm stuck with it by myself.
Twenty candles lit.
Illuminating my light.
Raising vibrations.
Hoping someone tunes into the frequency.

< Notes   ∨

raising vibrations, hoping someone tunes into the frequency, Notes

 Mitchell Paschall

to

May 19, 2013 Details

I'm in the dark, the lights are out, the energy bill got too expensive so we lost connection. In an abandoned building structured for two, solitude is less expensive. No reception through these walls either, the signals lost, 2nd party couldn't pay the cost, so I'm stuck wit it by myself. 20 candles lit, illuminating my light, raising vibrations, hoping someone tunes into the frequency,

 Mitch Paschall

to Allison

Mar 19, 2015 Details

---------- Forwarded message ----------

So in the end I gained a foe and not a friend.
But to hate would only let her win.

See it's hard to pretend that things are great.

When in the present state, you agitate and aggravate.

Not only physical wounds, but also mental, caused by a soul
that has been raped.
But wait, it is not my fault for placing faith in fake.
See fake was the want I never wanted to
want, but winded up wanting.
I don't think you understand, let me break it down.
Fake was that apple on the tree that looked so damn good.
A nigga just had to taste.
Knowing damn well that out of all the fruits in the garden,
That was the one I shouldn't take.

But by the time my conscience caught up with my actions,
it was too late.

Fake was the shark and I was the bait.
Well as the years evolved, my love increased.

Tears dissolved, my conscience deceased.
You tell me, was it peace or blinded bliss.

Throughout the course of our ship-lations relate,
Fake did some shit I just couldn't take.
"I swear to God, I swear on my life, I swear on my soul that
never again I'll cause you strife".

Well fake did so much swearing that you'd swear.
"I Swear", was the name of a fake who later became my plight.
But prior, I did my dirt. I told my lies.

I caused my hurts and brought forth cries.

So working it out, making it work became a guilted strive.
Loosing my self identity, forgetting my goals, sacrificing my
pride, emptying my soul,
Neglecting family, gaining weight, putting my dreams on
pause, losing faith,
Inhaling lies, swallowing deceit.

Making love to fake sighs, allowing my heart to pump to a
foreign beat.
All the while knowing she was lying through her teeth.
"I hate this shit, I'm done with your ass".

"Boy whatever, you need to get over it and leave the past in the past".

"Look can't you see by now that the past becomes present
if you don't correct the mistake that happened, last".

"I can't change who I am, I'm stubborn, I'm a Tarus".

"I'm not trying to hear all that, cause if you loved me,
you'd do it for us"

"Well I.. I"

"Just shut the hell up, I'm done talking, either you stop this
bullshit now or see me walking"
Well by this time your mind is constantly aching
from attempts at finding sympathetic justification.

Or translations of a relation in deprecation,
Causing so much depredation, ending in consternation.
Lord help me no one knows what I'm facing.
Outweighing the bad with the good.

But too much good without bad is bad.
And sometimes what's bad might be good.

Fake now has me second guessing.

Not knowing up from down, down from up.

I go to my mans, I call my moms, even my grandma,
and they all say "MAN YOU FUCKED UP"
Loving her had become an addiction.

A habit that at first I didn't realize.

But ever since my mom left me for her addictions.
Me feening for affection would become my demise.
And like a fool I stayed.
True she was fine as fuck.

And it had a nigga struck.

For some odd years, had a nigga stuck.

And for what, but tears and busting a few nutts.

Should have listened to my peers, never trust a smile with
a big butt.
But eventually I grew exhausted, being weak, and being fake.
Well, fake showed her ass off and did some shit I just
couldn't take.
It truly hurts now that I can see that while my love
continued to grow.
Fake, faked her way through and her love died a long time ago.

Moving at a swift paste and an anxious haste.

Fake indulged in a hidden taste.
As time went on, I grew strong becoming less and less obsessed.

Accomplished many goals, proving that endurance is the
key to success.

Looking back on all that pain, and realizing it was all just a test.

That God was only strengthening me and for that I'm blessed.

So while you've all been reading, my life is what I've
confessed to you.

I've already chewed up what was fake, so what I spit out is the truth.

A river still flows even when it falls.
Traces of summer are scenes even in the fall.
The sun is light even as a star.
Pain is felt without leaving scars.
A rainbow can be seen no matter where you are.
Dreams can be wished even from afar.
The sound of music is heard even when it's paused.
Love will flourish no matter the cause.

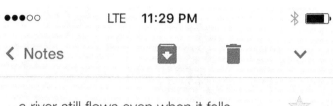

< Notes

a river still flows even when it falls,
traces of Notes

 Mitchell Paschall
to
Oct 17, 2013 Details

a river still flows even when it falls, traces of summer are scenes even in the fall, a sun is light even as a star, pain is felt without even a scar, a rainbow can be seen no matter where you are, dreams can be wished even from a far, the sound of music is heard even when it's paused, love will flourish no matter the cause ✌ & ♡ 1 ♥ 1 love

Edit Draft

Leaving our bodies for a moment.
Allowing our souls to experience the rhythm of the song.
Moving along the tones, finding each nuance.
Bringing us closer.
The beat building and dropping as
our hearts find synchronicity.
Bodies become closer.
So close that there's now just one body.
We move in unison.
The music and our souls become poetic.
Our limbs bending and folding into one another.
You look back.
I look in your eyes as we feel the confirmation that it's real.
The music has taken control.
The energy in the room has fueled this
escape into melodic hypnosis.
Aware of becoming unaware.
But we don't care.
We let go.
We just move.
We dance.

I put my heart into a lie.
I always thought I knew what's in your eyes.
Released my dreams into an open sky.
But now I see it was all empty cries.
And when you left you left with all the shine.
And I know in due time it will all be fine.
But for now.

Rain down on me girl now.
Rain down on me girl now.
Rain down on me girl now.

Let me experience remorse, show me some justification,
while my heart steadily aching.
Just a little precipitation could be your only reciprocation.

An ending storm with no silver line,
No present future, unless we go back in time.
Until the stars realign, and you find what's yours
And I find what's mine.
But for now.

Rain down on me girl now.
Rain down on me girl now.
Rain down on me girl now.

My frown could turn up from down,
If only I saw you cry now.

We were made in the image of the who has no image.
Infinite's expression, infinitely expressing.
Out of love and through the beauty of
creating, so therefore both are blind.
Fear not of what has been created to
define that which is undefinable.
It is the fabric threaded from origin, that makes us
originally love and beauty.

We were made in the image
of The who has no image.
Infinite's expression, infinitely
expressing. Out of love and
through the beauty of creating, so
there for both are blind. Fear
not of what has been created to
define that which is undefinable.
It is the fabric threaded from
Origin, that makes you originally
love and beauty

Mitchell Paschall

You're constantly reaching for me. Infinitely in effort to connect with me, your humble grace and loving desire to maintain the awareness that you're always present is the most righteous. It's the acknowledgement that one becomes conscious to, when the effort is reciprocated.

My Heavenly Father, how generous, how merciful thou has been to send signals and confirmation, to reinforce and encourage my divine pursuit. I love you Father. I see you, beyond the realms of me. The world is your reflection.

A gentle - man that's what I am.
A King amongst kings is what I've always been.
Aiming to love but always ready to defend.
No need to forcefully project my masculinity,
No need to pretend.
For I know exactly who I am.
Taking my kindness for weakness is only your mistake.
Cause what lies beneath your exterior is all that I want to awake,
You push me in hopes that I'll push you back just to test me.
Just grab my testis.
And you'll see there's no time for that.
Walking with my heart on my sleeve in a world filled
with snakes.
To me that's the bravest challenge a man can take.
I may not raise my voice when you think the time is right.
But ask anyone who knows me, I've never ran from a fight.
Choosing love over war has become my plight.
So I let relationships sail and birds fly like kites.
This King here has but only a true Queen in his sights.

In the end we might discover it was only the beginning.
That where we thought we started,
Was really a finish.
Descending into ascending dimensions.
While all along pretending misconceptions.
Lending our souls for eternal compensation.
Just to evolve.
And to elevate into secret reunions and relations.

Every negative thought that you have in you, you've decided to accept. You have allowed it to become a part of your identity, or how you perceive the world based on what you've seen in the world. But you know that it is all in illusion. The only thing that is real is what you feel is real, is what you think is real. The world and life have shown you multiple plethora of feelings and ideas. You simply choose that one that is representative of you. If you want to think you are these negative things, then you shall be. But if you think you are all these positive things then you shall be.

There are forces in this world, in this life who want to monopolize greatness, glory, freedom, wealth. So therefore many of us have been tricked into believing that we can only be less than what we already are. Denying the true truth that we are far more than what we can imagine. Only when man can imagine himself being more than what he is or more than what he sees, and creates whatever it is that he imagines, then we shall all be great like the greatness that created man.

We were in love if only for a moment.
If only for a moment, you really meant you love me.
If only for a moment, I could see you as my wife.
If only for a moment, we shared this life.
If only for a moment, this moment was just a moment.
Then maybe right now this would feel right.

We spent everyday together baby, we only left after night.
Loving each other became our addiction shorty.
But neither of us could ever take flight.
And you told me you love my passion.
Then I told you I love your action.
Infatuation got us over reacting.
Making vows, maybe just to hear how it sounds.
Not caring bout the future, just caring bout now.
Loving you, loving me, loving you,loving mean.
Got me feeling some type of way.

Some type of way.
You got me feeling.
You got me feeling.
Some type of way.

And you never thought you'd feel like this.
And I never thought again I'd be tricked.
But it's some shit you can't dismiss.
And sex like this you don't wanna miss.

You got me.
You got me feeling,
Some type of way.

Reflecting on all the things we said.
No body wants to evenly own it.
Now saying all the things unsaid.
Who could imagine where it would lead to.
No me and you or you and me , we hate them both.
Just waiting now for this moment to pass too.
If only for a moment, this moment wasn't a moment.
Then maybe what we felt first could last through.

Don't text me, I won't call you.
You got me feeling.
Some type of way.
You got me feeling.
Some type of way.

And you never thought you'd feel like this.
And I never thought again I'd be tricked.
But it's some shit you can't dismiss.
And sex like this you don't wanna miss.

You got me.
You got me feeling,
Some type of way.

And maybe we'll find forgiveness, but not today.
Not today.

You've gone away.
And I'm ok.
It's fucked up, it ended that way.

The ocean allows moments to listen.
And the sky lets each star glisten.
Might we go back to that moment of
eye contact before kissing.
When I discovered what was missing.
My heart insisting it was you..
My mind dismissing the truth.
Each night listening.
Your voice whispering.
Through moist lips, slithering.
As I fall deep, deep into your love.
And like the shooting star, diving into the ocean.
My soul chose this life in devotion.
Let the ecstasy we create be the token.
Buying enough time to spend eternity
invoking all that is love.
All that is pure, for it is the presence of God that allures.
So as we let space and time be our cure.
Might I take this moment in rhyme
to remind, that you my love,
Is all that I adore.

It was the summer of 2007. I was nearing the end of my year break from Cali, which started spring of 2006. I had left LA and moved back to Baltimore for a year just to clear my head. Wayne was just bodying everything! I mean *"The Carter 2"* carried us through all of '06, then he dropped *"The Drought 3"* right in time for summer 07!

By the time Dj Khalid, *"We Taking Over"* dropped, **maaan** I just had to hop on something. After I heard Wayn kill this, I was motivated to try it out. I had a whole lot to get off my chest. That was a very pivotal point in my life, one of the most trying, but also most rewarding. This was my first written rap Ever in life!!

Ayo, here we go, it's ya boy P-shells repin Baltimore,
If you wanna talk shit, we can go to war,
tough niggas pull clips and be really hores,
I'm not what you looking for,
if you wanna crack slick what you waiting for,
you'll do a back flip from this 44,
don't you know I eat beef like I'm starving poor
Un un, no no you didn't underestimate me cause I'm far from finished
Took a long break son, but now I'm replenished
Shorty couldn't keep it real she was hard to distinguish
Grew tired of what was fake so I had to relinquish
Tried to damage my heart but now she's diminished

And yes and yes it feels so splendid,
so excuse me for three minutes to use rap to vent with
So wait I admit I lost my pace,
I lost my grace maybe even lost a lace
but I kept on running never quitting the race
cause I stayed mad hungry never losing my taste
And I won't ever exit, not until a nigga use all that he blessed with
Impulsive blows niggas can't mess with
Compulsive flows is how I express it
Y'all fake MC stink like hot farts and fruity like pop tarts
Man fuck the pop charts let's bring real hip hop back for the culture
I said I'd kill it so I stabbed it
Addicted to the track like an addict
I wear the beat tight like a jacket
Spitting out flames leaving nothing but ashes
And ask this when it comes to hot flows who can match this
I'm not your same ordinary more than average
Got jammed got tested and I lasted everlasting
One of the baddest fell down bounced back like Elastic
the wrong words might get ya ass blasted
the wrong move might put you in a casket
You stupid bastard
And tip top flip flop ya sticky stump
Loose lips pop trunks pulling out a pretty pump
Don't stop kick rocks you little chump
Click clocking the glock is not what you really want
I eat more than enough threats just for breakfast and shots after
shots just for brunch
So home boy if you really feeling reckless for war
Then I'll see you for lunch

Or maybe a glass of punch but I really hate to see ya head
blown like a conch
Go ahead bring a bunch I munch crews
You can call me captain crunch
Then I'll take ya bags, take ya jag
Pull off and roll up a really fat blunt
Didn't I already mention once
I'm from B-more baby niggas here don't stunt
But don't blame me for being violent
I'm only a product of my environment
Mom and dad couldn't do the job early retirement
Became a badass youth way too defiant
Always in trouble for not being silent
Instead of running scared we ran to the sirens
Hide and go freak was how our summer spent
Nick or knock hopping over the fence
Sneaking mad sips of ya uncles old E
Tryna to get bent only made you dizzy
Corner store stealing hot butter bean
Smacking round feens now they chasing me
Smashing JLo was my fantasy
School detention screaming give us us free
Hitn the roach only made you choke
Little bad ass niggas taking more than they can tote
And so I wrote
And so I spoke
All the pain in my brain
Encouraging hope
Maintain being sane
Just trying to cope

Paying the price of wanting fame
So now I'm broke
Staying focused in my lane
Never swerving nope
Slinging these words and these verbs
In exchange for dope
Play the game til my fame
Change the status-quo
Is my focus and my aim
Better yet my oath
All the soil and all the rain
Only gave me growth
I had a gut and a lust
So I lost them both
About a foot from the edge
Yeah I came real close
Almost lost my head
So I left that coast

In a life full of endless possibilities.
Within a world of uncertainties.
I'm just saying, one day maybe, I could call you baby.

As the past falls further and further behind you.
And those in the rear view,
Become sublime too.
Manifesting into me & you.
Maybe then you'll let me call you baby.

While we're entwined in organic rhythms of our souls.
Where halves become whole.
The reunion of twin flames.
Separated at the dawn of existence.
Joining only to restore harmonic consistence.
I'm just saying can a nigga call you baby.

Each day passes by, only bringing familiarities.
The words that manipulate their way off my lips.
Come nowhere close to expressing the bliss ,
That exists when just in your presence.
And at present.
I reminisce how seconds ago I observed melancholy
amongst your aura.
Wishing my eyes told you "I'm here for ya baby".
See it wasn't that bad, was it baby?.

Open your heart and let me get to work.
Reconstructing your veins of pain, removing all the hurt.
Let my voice softly whisper in your ear.
Numbing you from any fear.
If only you'd embrace all this love.
That is so clear.

With the passion of PAC, sweet Sadie.
I'll bomb on any nigga trying hurt my baby.
My baby, a Queen of a Lady.
When will you realize that I'm real.
Filled with God's Light, so far from being shady.

Maybe it'll all end with you saying "this niggas crazy".
Or you'll look within, and say " yeah.. I'll be your baby".
One day... I'm just saying ... maybe??

Words would be cliches.
So like heights that birds soar each day.
In my mind are sights of you that I replay.
Your views are venues.
The Creators art on display.
So I pause and hover.
As I discover you.
You.
You,
Your natural hue.

The love you spew.

WORDS WOULD BE CLICHE
SO LIKE HEIGHTS THAT
BIRDS SOAR EACH DAY
IN MY MIND ARE SIGHTS
OF YOU THAT I REPLAY
YOUR VIEWS ARE VENUES
THE CREATORS ART ON DISPLAY
SO I PAUSE AND HOVER
AS I DISCOVER YOU,
        YOU,
        YOU,
        YOUR NATURAL HUE
        THE LOVE YOU SPEW . . .

May it pour, cleansing away yesterday's sorrows.
Overflowing the pail of today's and tomorrow's.
So we might stand drenched in now.
Thirst quenched, like a moist french kiss,
And the only thing we starve for is more, more, more.
Mother's perspiration absorbing into our veins.
Sustaining all life, relinquishing pain and strife.
Like in the form of a flame matched.
Like the sun.
Like birth.
Like earth.
Like love.
Like cycles.
Hi.
And hi again.
Endless rain.

'MAY it pour, cleansing away
yesterdays sarrows
OVER flowing the pail of today's
and tomorrow's
So we might stamd drenched
In (rows)

THIRST Quenched like a moist
french kiss
And the only thing we starve for
is MORE MORE MORE
Mothers's perspiration absorbing
Into our veins
Sustaining all LIFE
Relinquishing pain and strife
Like in the form of A flame matched
Like the sun
Like birth
Like earth
Like LOVE ♡
Like cycles) HI ☺
AND HI again
ENDLESS RAIN

Can a conscious nigga just smash too?
I'm really not trying to disrespect you.
Or neglect ya feelings, I know you
only deal with a select few.
But we ain't gotta build a whole lot,
Just for me to knock down ya walls if you don't need to.
You're probably thinking that I'm well read.
Different cloth, eclectic patterns,
Woven threads.
But look,
Even with a book,
Sometimes, you gotta first crack the spine,
Just so the pages easily spread.
I'm just saying....
No pressure here.
What you truly desire is so clear.
But your assumptions of what I think.
Has caused your fears.
Maybe in the past some lame caused your name to smear.
Fuck that nigga.
No one really cares.
Wait, but I know you do.
So allow me to confess, undressing the truth
of what I want to address to you.
Goddess,
I wanna do more than
impress you.

I wanna bless you.
Discover ya flavors.
Light savors.
Like lifesavers.
Release your stress too.
All I'm saying is, It's just me and you.
And I know I sound pressed.
But you could've been left.
So what you trying to do?
Oh word.
Say less?
You called the Lyft too?

I can now admit that I've always had a problem dealing with reality, or should I say my personal perception of reality. From a young age, I can recall the beginning of me trying to escape. While all the other children would play outside for many hours, you could find me watching movies back to back. In those moments, I was truly internalizing those cinematic experiences, not realizing that this constant programming was shaping my entire perception of life. I turned to television to avoid the bitterness of my life, hiding from drug abusing parents, abandonment, alcoholism and severe domestic violence.

Along with those traumas, I also could never fit into the two different worlds I had to face. In catholic school, I wasn't white enough and in the projects I wasn't black enough. The exhaustion from this attempt led me to retreat into silence and further entering into fantasy worlds. Shows and movies like the Cosby's, The Goonies, Disney and Indiana Jones had become my refuge. I remember my first attempt at trying to get a girlfriend was in first grade, and I created an elaborate plan to accomplish this. The plan was to have Bernard and Adam tease Stacey and her friends, then I would swing in from my imaginary rope to rescue her; this would make her fall in love with me and become my first girlfriend. My plan was a total disaster. The three of us got in trouble and loss recess for a week.

I guess this is one of the reasons I fell in love with acting. Acting would allow me to safely and acceptingly indulge into an entirely different reality. Fast forward to age thirty one, I can see the correlation and the effects of many years of conditioning. Many experiences I've created have been dramatic, cinematic or Disney-ish.

Although I might have become one of the most optimistic people in the world, many things I have ran away from. I can also say that I've missed many signs and misjudged people due to my pure ignorance and subconsciously rejection of reality. I became a man this year when I woke up to all the harshness, to the reality that I was escaping all my life. Noticing how disheartening it still is, I now have told myself, "it's all good and it's gonna be what it's gonna be. In life, we must experience it the best way we can, with what we have. We work hard to change our reality and only then can we can change the world.

Mitchell Paschall
March 24 at 12:38pm ·

I can now admit that I've always had a problem dealing with reality, or should I say my own perception of my personal reality. From a young age I can now recall the beginnings of me escaping it. While all the children would play outside for many hours through out the day, you could find me watching movies back to back to back, and for those moments I would be living those cinematic experiences, not realizing that this constant programming was shaping my perception on actual life. As I turned to television to avoid the bitterness of my real life, drug abusing parents, abandonment, alcoholism, severe domestic violence and never quite fitting in two different environments. In the projects I wasn't hood enough and in Catholic school I wasn't white enough, after exhaustion of pleasing both, I soon retreated to silence and disappearing into a fantasy world, with the Cosbys, The Goonies, Disney and Indiana Jones. As a matter of fact my first attempt on trying to ask a girl out; was in first grade and the plan was to get my best friend Adam Lee, and Bernard to tease and harass Stacey and her friends and then I would swing in from my imaginary rope, beat them up and save Stacey,

friends and then I would swing in from my
imaginary rope, beat them up and save Stacey,
thus making her fall in love with me and
becoming my first girlfriend, needless to say it
was a disaster. We all got in trouble and lost
recess for the rest of the week. I guess this is
one of the reasons I fell in love with acting, it
allowed me to guilt free indulge into a entirely
different reality no matter how extreme and it be
accepted in the collective reality. Fast forward at
31 I see the correlation and effect of many years
of this conditioning. Many experience I've
created, have been dramatic, cinematic, or
Disney-ish. Although I might have become one
of the most optimistic people in the WORLD,
and my pure ignorance or subconsciously
rejecting reality, many things I've ran away from,
many signs I have missed, people I've viewed
from only one point of view instead of there
entire spectrum. I became a man this year when
I woke up to all the harshness, to the reality that
I was escaping all my life and saw how
hardening it still is, and said to my self, " it's all
good, I can handle it, It is what is, its gona be
what's gona be" "in life we must experience it
the best way we can with what we have" "Work
hard to change your world your reality and once
you've change your world your reality, only then
can you change The World.

As a boy I ran my first marathon at ten. I had no formal training, knowledge of pace or even comprehend how far 3k was. So like any boy anxious to show off in competition, when it started, I jetted out at full speed. I looked back moments later and saw the other runners slowly jogging, I was confused, but felt overly confident. I soon realized why they were taking their time after about 100 yards in. Before I was halfway around the lake, runners were passing me, one by one. As I watched them ahead of me, I felt so discouraged. But I told myself, no matter what I was going to finish. I finished, beyond exhausted, and walked away with a valuable lesson. I experienced the difference between a race and a marathon.

Most endeavors in life are or should be characterized as a marathon. A starting point & finishing point that you pace through at your own time. The only thing that matters is that you don't stop and that you finish. God awakened me in 2012, giving me a seductive and addicting taste of euphoria, supreme connection with Him and all that exists. Life for a couple weeks looked and tasted different, epiphanies of all measures were delivered as I totally emerged my being into this spiritual enlightenment. I began reading stacks of books, meditating, changing my diet and making every attempt to stay in tune with God, it was the highest of highs. It was better than weed, alcohol even sex!

But eventually that initial sensation like when you first hit the weed, it's effect began to lessen. And all this time I've been desperately trying to get it back. Sprinting my way into obtaining pure enlightenment, reaching for the crown chakra, nirvana. And I grew tired and exhausted cause I wasn't reaching the finish line as fast as I could. Didn't pace myself, or establish **BALANCE!!!** I just wanted to be totally emerged in God, filled with love and light from head to toe constantly. Yet to obtain this, you have to realize it's not a race but a lifelong marathon. And to be honest one that obtains this, probably would no longer need to experience this physical reality. But there's work to be done through me in this physical form, so we live to learn, balance and pace ourselves through life's marathon, in pursuit of *Divine Enlightenment*. By the time we are finished in this life, in this form, we all shall obtain it. Namaste, peace and love, one love, one heart.

I don't understand.
I'm lost and confused.
I want to give up.
But my heart continues to refuse.
My mind is tortured and constantly abused.
Where will I end up?
On top or at the bottom.
There isn't much time,
I have no patience for my loss of motivation.
I just have hope and sporadic enthusiasm.
The force in my strides are inconsistent.
I have no hope but much persistence.
How will I land?
Backwards ?
So I won't know when the end is coming.
Or forward?
So I can have a split second to briefly reminisce.
It is best to run without thought.
Time to question only distance you from actually doing something.
When will I finally win this traitorous race?
I must know now because I'm losing my pace.
03/11/02

Rewritte 3/11/02
6:55 pm

3/23/02
Homeless

I don't understand
I'm lost and confused
I want to give up;
But my heart continues to refuse
My mind is tortured & constantly aroused
Where will I end up
On top or at the bottom
There isn't much time
I have no patience for my
lack of motivation
I just have hope and sporadic enthusiasm
The force in my strides are inconsistent
I have no hope but much persistence
How will I land
Backwards or I won't know then who and
will hit me
Or forward, so I can have split second
to briefly remains
It's best to run with quiet thoughts
Time it question only distance you
from actually doing
When will I finally win this treacherous race
I must know now; because I'm loosing
my pace

I really don't have much to say.
Because lately things haven't been okay.
Not saying that they ever are.
But worse because some things that
appeared to be close, now seem far.
It feel as if the building that I started,
Has now been broken up and parted.
My life is starting to change rapidly, so I try to keep up.
But there are always hurdles that cause me to trip and mess up.
See I have been running a race all my time living.
So long that I can't even see myself winning.
But being the determined person that I am.
I can't give up and just put the struggle to an end.
Because the only thing that is going to get me to the finish line.
Is the ego and the constant urge to win, that is all mine.
I got this characteristic from no one else.
That's why things that happen for me must be done by myself.
And when I finally do win the race.
I will slow down and continue to live my life at a steady pace.
But until I win.
The only encouraging thoughts I need to get through life.
Is to win, win, win.

Spare of the moment 4/22/99

4/10/99

Spare of the Moment 4/22/99

I really don't have much to say
Because lately things haven't been okay

Not that they ever are
But worse because some things that
appeared to be able to reach, now
seem far

It feels as if the building that I have
started,
Has now been broken up and parted

My life is starting to change rapidly
So I try to keep up
But there are always hurdles in my
pathway that cause me to trip and
mess up.

See I have been running a race all
my time living.
So long that I can't even seeing
myself winning

But being the determined person
I am I can't give up and just put
the struggle to an end.

Because the only thing that is
going to get me to the finish line
Is me the ego and the constant
ego to winning that is, all mine

I got this characteristics from
no one else
Thats why things that happen
for me, must be done by myself

And when I finally do win the
race.
I will slow down and continue
my life at a steady pace

But until I win
The only encouraging thoughts
I need to get through life
Is to win win win!.

At a moment's moment one could be captured in forever.
If so let forever be dined with she who dawned at my existence.
No cliche meant to be, but a forsaken must be.
Desirable for one's own completion.
If treason be by he who reasons with clear love.
Then may disdained love and
uncertainties remain in the depths of my past.
And remain at the end of my demise.
For I will awake and arise at her calling .
Falling for love yet once again.
Her battered heart need not take mercy on me.
Her toughened spirit need not hold blows.
Like a tailored suit, I was made for her.
Created to sustain her pains.
Quiet her storms.
And tranquil her angers and frustrations.
My motivation is her emancipation.

Mitchell Paschall
to
Dec 3, 2012 Details

At a moment's moment, one could be captured in forever, if so let forever be dined with she who dawned at my existence. No cliché meant to be, but a forsaken must be, desirable for ones own completion. If treason be by he who reasons with clear love, than may disdained love & uncertainties remain in the depths of my past and remain at the end of my demise. For I will await and rise at her calling, falling for love yet once again, her battered heart need not take mercy on me, her tainted soul need not shy from me, her toughened spirit need not hold blows, like a tailored suit, I was made for her, created to Sustain her pains. Quite her storms and tranquil her angers and frustration, my motivation is her emancipation.

I closed my eyes once and whispered for something more.
Not sure where this longing came from, or even imagine
it's cure. Then I met a girl on a distant shore from a distant shore.
Her pure heart touched my core, leaving me longing no more.
Only filled, restoring my faith, with so much hope for
what's in store.

But time moves us forward, distancing us more,
Even though my heart yearns to detour.
Taking me back to the night, when I was blessed to explore,
A Goddess, looking at her, thinking to myself..
"How I deserve all this!"
Each caress on her skin each kiss on her body.
I could only wish that a second lasted for minutes
And each minute was an hour and an hour was a lifetime.
Delighted to dine with such divine,
My head is trapped, behind and abreast.
And I attest, dare I say more, it would only be of less,
Than all that I could truly confess.

So my memories lay in secret, like an egg in a nest.
Awaiting to hatch, awaken to latch.
Clinging to her love.
The beating in our chest becomes indistinguishable .
A passionate fire that's inextinguishable.
Even as I try to paint the picture with words,
It's still unexplainable.

I mean it's crazy.
Absurdities.
Palpable courtesies.
A mending man, placed in her hands.
Her conviction reminded me of who the fuck I am.
This Queen performs multiple bypass surgeries.
By passing love you see.
Purposefully for me.

And I'm no selfish man, so I give more back than what's given.
Replenishing a sacred soul of all the energy she was sending.
So much that she's been restored,
and there's still more pending.
Never ending galore.
Cause I've learned the best way to obey
ya thirsts is by pouring more into your woman.

So in lending time and space .
The Universe gifts us time to retrace.
When two aligning stars embraced in a foreign place.
When we were truly living our best life.
So many answers were revealed.
Certainly those nights destiny was fulfilled .

And so until, we meet again,
My lover my friend, I'm constantly wishing
You love and contentment.
And may God bless you manifesting
All your commitments and may it be relentless.
For there is nothing that He can't do.

And through you,
He's solidified that any doubts I have,
Ain't true.
So thank you, thank you, thank you!
In my heart you live... and so it is.

"The five stages to self love"

1. Discovery (of self)

2. Deciding (of self)

3. Accepting (self)

4. Embracing (self)

5. Falling in love (with self)

There comes that moment in life when we may begin to explore. One may tiptoe out of personal perimeters, whether physically or mentally. And based upon these first initial steps or how strong one's personal conditioning are, it determines whether to continue or retreat. It's the innate curiosity of asking oneself, 'how far can I go' combined with the true hidden desire of the rebellious spirit that exists in all. When we realize that life is all about exploring and expanding, and we're not bound by society, family expectations or circumstances, then we begin to discover self.

{ *DEFINITE SELF* } I.e... loyal, sensitive hearted, heterosexual...

No one is ever lost. Or in search of finding themselves. It's truly a matter of defining or redefining oneself. It's the spirit that speaks to your conscience, saying " look, we have been this way for sometime, and it's not working, it doesn't resonate entirely, let's make some alterations or lose it all together ". We must keep in mind however that this defining or for the better **REFINING**, is constant. Everything is in a state of expanding, learning and growing.

At first I was feeling very disappointed with myself. Like I let myself down. Simultaneously appreciating the many gifts last night's experience offered. I still feel foolish in retrospect thinking that I may have said too much, revealed battling insecurities and quite frankly embarrassed myself. But life goes on. I saw your true essence and I fell in love with you again or I fell in love with another side of you. Realizing also that I've begun to fall in love with love instead of enjoying „*You*", my set back quickly becomes a step forward. An obsession that I thought was fully addressed. Quickly striking me with bombardment of epiphanic growth, I digress but in balance.

Overwhelmed with this emotion and sensation, one falls into the trap of handling it with old tools from a previous garden, rusted and abandoned. But what do you do when a new garden emerges out of the blue and you're left born new. Whatever it is, I just don't want to lose you. So I'll pump the fuck out my breaks. Began manifesting the most immaculate tools, using all that I've learned and plant new seeds accompanied with you. Please forgive me for drowning you with my love, affection and emotions. I have so much love inside of me; my children can't handle it, and my niggas can't comprehend it.

I try to release to as many throughout the day, but a new love is forced to take it all. I'm sorry. I'm scared and as a man I'm supposed to be sure. I'm supposed to be balanced,

I'm supposed to be solid. But yet I'm being exploded and reconstructed simultaneously. In my eager attempt to sweep you off your feet, God and your existence is sweeping me off mine. I don't want to lose you before I get the chance to have you.

My ending conclusion is that last night was supposed to happen, God makes no mistakes. My heart wants to reel you in, but my heart wants to push you away, to prevent any potential heart ache. All the while you sit in loud silence. I know now you know far far more than you show, your intelligence, awareness is delivered tactfully, causing suspicion. Is it selfish for me to wish everyone lived naked like me. Truth of the matter, I am strong, I am extremely motivated, ambitious, goal oriented, focused , and disciplined. God just help a nigga. You know my heart is in your light's direction.

Incense burning, the smoke dancing in the air.
As the wind blows through the window.
Gradually she disappears.
OH...,
How hypnotic are her rhythmic moves.
Trapping eyes of lust, may make you mistrust.
Any view from your perspective.
Her scent of perfume may have caused the only deception.
Inhaling the sweet tasted of mass masked misconceptions.
Clouded thoughts then brought all sorts of distortion.

Incense burning, the smoke dancing in the air, as   Notes

Mitchell Paschall
to
Aug 24, 2014 Details

Incense burning, the smoke dancing in the air, as the wind blows thru the window gradually she disappears oh.,, hypnotic are her so rythmatic moves. Trapping eyes of lust, may make you mistrust, any view from your perspective, her sent of perfume may have caused the only deception, inhaling the sweet taste of mass masked misconceptions, clouded thoughts, then brought all sorts of distortion

Reply

Forward

In Loving Memory of Aaliyah about 11:00 am 8/29/01

I guess it's true about what they say, you never appreciate something until it's gone. It's a shame that I and many others didn't recognize your true beauty until you left to never return again. I now regret that I slept. Ignoring all of your talent and potential. Not realizing that there was a lot of skill that you possessed, that was just starting to blossom and open up to the world. I apologize for you and all the others.

I try to answer the question of why don't people cry when everyday people die, but when someone like you is taken from this world many shed tears. I've come to the **"RESOLUTION"** that tears are a secret thing, most only cry when something truly strikes them. Society builds a callus for everyday tragedies. After getting struck by the same hit or punch, your body becomes used to it. You soon become able to endure the beatings you receive, making pain bearable.

I slept on your beauty and all the uniqueness you possessed. I was sleeping while you were flourishing the world with your gifts. Now I try to keep from weeping.

Highway 1/24/01
11:49AM

The first time I got high
was a feeling like no other
I thought of all the good things
that I felt, but then began
thinking about my mother.
So it gives you emotional
feelings one after another.

But you can control it once
you are able to discover

these sensations wavering makin
that slow down your pulse
is

In loving memory of Elijah
about 11:0? on 8/29/01

I guess its true what they say
you never appreciate something til
it's gone. It's a shame that I
and many others died recognize
your true beauty until you left
to never return again.

I now regret the fact
The fact that I slept

Ignoring all of you talent and
potential
Not realizing that there was
alot of skill that you possess
that was just starting to blossom
and open up to the world.
I apologize for you and all
the others.

I try to answer the question
of why don't people cry
when everyday people die
but when someone like you
is taken from this world

many shed tears, & come
up with the "resolution"
that tears are a secret thing,
men only cry when something
truly affects them, society
~~builds~~ builds a callous
for its every day tragedies,
after getting stitch but
to some but in over you,
body becomes use to it,
you soon become able to
endure the beating, you
recieve) making pain bearable.

I ~~truly~~ truly regret the
fact that & did it.

Slept in your beauty
and all the universe you
poses)

I was pleasure while you
were flourishing the world with
your self.

now I try to keep from
wearing

Some time in 2002

I guess that as humans we are never satisfied. We are so spoiled and ungrateful, that we can't see that everything that we need is right under our noses. We don't realize that we have what we want, but don't even want what we have.

Our minds can only see what others possess. Jealousy and envy pollutes our thoughts, shaping our personal imagination. Soon, within our mind, body and souls; we become a replica of a false illusion of a true reflection. We may think that this is who we are, not knowing that it is someone else. To accept what is given and use it to as an advantage is a great virtue. To always wish for more is ignorance. One is born beautiful, watered and nourished in order to blossom. The wrong amount of exposure allows weeds to grow.

There is a thin line between needing and wanting. To want perhaps is the lowest denomination of need. What is want? Could it be irrelevant? Since there are but only a few things that a human being really needs in order to live.

I guess, that as humans we
are never satisfied
We are so spoiled and ungrateful
that we can't see that everything
that we need is right under our nose.
We don't know or realize that
we have want we want, but don't
want what we have.
Our minds can see only what
others poses, jealousy and envy
pollute out thoughts, choking
our own personal imagination.
Soon become in mind, body
& soul, a replica of a false
illusion of a true reflection.
We may think that this is
who we really are, but not
realizing that it is someone else.
To accept accept what is given,
and using it to an advantage,
is a great virtue.

To always wish for more is ignominious.

One is born with beauty, water and nourished, as a seed to blossom into a beautiful flower, but with the wrong amount of exposure, they become weeds.

There is a thin line, I must agree, between needing and wanting. To want perhaps is to the lowest denomination, or to need. But what is need? Could need be irrelevant since there are but a few things that humans really do need in order to live.

I'm not sure if it was when I was ten years old or before? I remember going to the movies with my father to see "Boyz n the Hood". That was in 91, so I was eight years old. I can recall the night he held me for the first time, embracing me, making me feel loved and comfortable. That was the night we went late night fishing and got into a very bad accident. We were sitting in the grass waiting for the ambulance. He just held me between his legs, rocking me back and forth. Saying to me, "It's going to be ok".

I can still see the big flash of light before the big impact. It had to have been around the time we were driving in his red 89 honda prelude, man I loved that car! The soft black upholstery, with the car freshener scent mixed with cigarette aroma, I could ride in the front seat for days. But the day that stood out the most around this period was when I was riding in the back seat. My father asked me to call him dad. Which shortly followed the day I visited him in rehab. Like my mother, my father also fell victim to drug addiction.

The fight for avoiding addiction started very early for me. Between witnessing one parent and experiencing the void and absence of another, I quickly identify the traits that I must master and be cautious of. But no one was there to warn me of how addiction could disguise itself in other forms.

I set the bar extremely high, with clear intentions at an early age, never do drugs, drink alcohol or smoke cigarettes. So what does a kid with ptsd and emotional traumas do, who has set his attention on not becoming an addict? Well the first thing, as a reader you're experiencing it now. The second and third wasn't realized until many years later.

So presently at thirty-six, I'm the largest I've ever been; 5"5 and 220 pounds, **GOT DAMN**! Yeah say it out loud! I've been in a space where I've overcome cigarettes which I'd been smoking for 3 years and also broken the cycle of feening for love from everyone but myself. Which has left me with my very first and last addiction that I have to face, emotional eating. My weight has consistently fluctuated throughout my adult life. If I wasn't grounded by the determination of achieving an immediate goal, then it's likely I would slack off working out. But once my mind is made up, I'd quickly get in shape, whether it was for acting or football, just never purely for me. Being in shape had always been a by-product from accomplishing something else.

Fifth grade was my first run in with this addiction. I don't remember the exact triggers, but I remember for the majority of that year, I was going down stairs late at night and just going ham on junk. Eating apple pie and ice cream or a whole pack of double stuff Oreos late at night became a ritual. This felt good to me, took my mind off of whatever I was thinking about and it put me to sleep. The only thing that stopped this routine was my introduction to football in sixth grade. After my first day of practice, I fell in love! That was my new escape.

Football took me all the way to high school, where I met my second addiction, love and affection. It begins in tenth grade. My son's mother, girlfriend at the time gave me something I hadn't felt since I was about seven or eight years old. Something I forgot I needed and yearned for. She was loving, affectionate and caring the way my mother was. I quickly relied on her for self worth, validation and purpose. Placing such a heavy burden on a teenage girl still trying to figure her shit out. I turned to her love and attention like a newborn to a bottle. It was terrible.

It took many years and self realization to establish self worth and learn how to love myself. I had to go cold turkey with everything. I prayed, **PRAYED!** The type of prayer where I am trying to hold God hostage until I know in my soul he hears me. Um, as I'm writing that, I realized it's my **SOUL** making sure I hear it! And for real, for real God is making sure I hear **HIM!!** Man, I tell you... God loves me... SMH (*shaking my head*)! He loves you too! I'm only saying *"He"* out of habit, but y'all know what I mean.

So the spirit of addiction may have transferred into me because of my parents, or subconsciously it was learned behavior, whatever the case was, I went through it. When life got hard, I'd turn to a new way to pacify myself. I'd become numb to that and find another. From masturbation, cigarettes even short bouts with alcohol and weed, all these things I cling to in avoidance and escaping me. So that's where I am now, dealing with me.

I've been single for two years, and no sex for over two years. I've even done a couple 90 day nofaps. I'm learning how to be okay alone. I'm discovering different ways to love and appreciate myself. My confidence is no longer a pseudo, but genuinely reflecting an internal emotion. 2020 will begin a whole new decade and a promising new chapter in my life.

We hold on to the past in fear of the future.
Categorizing our mistakes in order to protect.
Neglecting the present.
A permanent resident.
Living in torment of what's to come.
We hold on to what has happened.

What you see in my eyes is nothing more than a reflection
of what you see in yours.
Poured endeavors and sore cores.
Blanket statements hurt more.
Is this not what we both searched for?
Must we go through life experiencing frequent infatuations.
She'll we have faith in the chemistry reminiscent of that
which we shared from a mother or father.
in this game called life there are no rules,
one rolls the dice cross their fingers
and hope not to get hurt twice .
Might we take a chance again,
or do we forever allow the hurt within,
to prevent a new love to begin.
Pain is what reminds us we are still alive
and what doesn't kill us only makes us stronger.
So my love for love only increases my hunger.
No longer will I completely empty myself into another.
A more balanced love is what we should desire for one another.
Gradually building like soft tones in a love song,
So when the beat drops you know when it's coming.
Never ending days that end.
So when apart we're missed again.
Both are evenly yoked.
Where we're able to breath, the opposite of being choked.
Two separate lives, living.
Simultaneously as one.

Barely experiencing growing pains.
Cause we're having too much fun.
Each level of our growth.
Only flourishes reciprocity.
As we invent a new love language.
The deck of cards has burned.
Total trust has been earned.
Speaking with words has become rudimentary.
For you are all the love I put out and was sent back to me.
Combined, we created a new energy.
Not confined by time, but intertwined in synchronicity.
And with ease and simplicity.
Pushing past thresholds,
as my patients only make you more anxious.
We ain't deep enough yet.
When I say I will always love you,
you now know it's a promise and not a threat.
Your light erased any shadows,
so you're walking only in your own steps.
Damn I'm blessed.
Keeping us moving forward.
Only looking back to tell me "it's yours".
Now when our eyes meet, our hearts soar.
For now we see this is what we've been waiting for.
Need I say more?

There is no right or wrong, only perception and perspective. You take religion out of the equation, and you just look at life and all the living physical aspects of it. What is the one true common denominator that every species strives for, their entire existence? Love. This is the core, everything stems from it, even hate.

Now look at things from a nonphysical perspective, in denial of a creator, or a source. One still has to question, what is responsible for such an intricate creation of everything that exists. What source created intelligent minds, planets, the operation of the stars, and the solar systems in which they govern?

The inner connection you feel with animals and mankind. How a dog can recognize negative energy in a person versus positive. Intuition, chakras and frequencies that have been scientifically proven to exist, matter- which everything consists of, in you and outside of you. What you see and don't see. "$E=mc2$"? So why not celebrate these things? Why not give thanks and praises to these things?

One doesn't even have to refer to these miraculous, loving, gracious, existence as God. But to ignore it and live blind, would be total ignorance and insanity. One naturally loves their mother, we give thanks and praise to her. Not the act of sexual intercourse; sperm, eggs etc, but the one who birth us. Why not do the same to the one or the what that birth every fucking thing? It's simple, when you're given a gift, what do you say? TEMET NOSCE!

I'm never not going to need you, God!
Is it ok for me to feel helpless, fragile,
handicapped without you?
It's crazy because I feel like I'm always crying for help,
I feel like a spoiled child always crying for their fathers help.
Like am I wrong for wanting to prove to you that
I can muscle through some things alone.
Do you see me as weak, spoiled, or lazy?
Did Jesus call upon you every single step of the way?
I sometimes feel like I have no right to cry to you,
to feel hurt or helpless because there's so many
of my brothers and sisters that are going through
or have gone through the worst.
And you **ANSWER ALL MY PRAYERS ALL THE TIME!!**
Like should I leave you alone and
let you tend to those that are in far greater pain than I?
I feel so selfish!
But I feel so stuck and helpless at times.
I have no right to complain or feel this way, it sickens me.
I'm fortunate.
Unfortunately so conflicted.

03/17/02
I'm full of decisions.
Right ones that later wrong themselves.
Wrong ones that later correct themselves
I am spent mostly trying to find why.
What am I?
Most would rather end me.
Then to spend time defining me.
I must admit wearing my large shoes is a very hard task.
Only those with courage and determination will last.
I was built to test the strength of all.
A long test created by the one some call God,
My purpose is that alone.
Because enduring me is ensuring that you will have a place
near his throne.
I am compared to a journey.
And sometimes a ride.
No matter what I am, no one can hide.
After a few years of experiencing me many break down and cry.
Who am I?
My essence is hard to reach.
My lessons are nearly impossible to teach.
I can't stop existing, I will remain in the form of many others,
Each and every soul gets the chance to bond with me.
Most try to blind themselves from me, from head to toe
in denial.
Not knowing I still remain in their presence all the while.

I occasionally take pity on the ones who get lost.
And take ease on the ones who were born
with the need for a frequent pause,
I am a non existing existence.
A surrounding that has no decadence.
I am simply here to provide.
Who am I?

3/19/62

I'm full of decisions
right ones that better correct themselves
and wrong ones that later wrong
themselves
& am spent mostly trying to find why
What am I
Most would rather end me
Then to spent the majority of time deporting
me
I must admit wearing my large shoes
is a merey hard task
Only thoughts with courage and
determination will last
I was built to test the strengths
of all, a long list created by
the one some would call God
My purpose is that alone
Because enduring me
insuring that the one
will have place near his throne
I am compare to a journey
And sometimes a ride

No matter what I am no one
is able to hide
After a few years of experiencing me
many break down and cry
What am I
My essence is hard to reach
My lessons are nearly impossible to
teach
I can't stop existing, I will remain
unbroken in the form of many others
Each and every soul gets the chance
to bond with me, most try
to blind themselves from life
Ripping themselves from head to toes
in denile
Not knowing I still remain in their
present all the while
Occasionally take pity on
the ones who get lost
And take ease on the ones who were
born to me with the need for a
constant pause

∞ I am a non existing
existence
The surroundings that has
decadence
no circumstances
I am simply here to parade
What am I

I am light?
I am light!
That's what I've discovered
Or at least what I've been told.
Light.
I'm fifty pounds overweight.
I don't feel light.
I'm constantly trying to blend in the dark.
You know, walk in the shade.
But I'm supposed to be light.
Formed in the dark.
Born into the light,
but surrounded by darkness
with distant specks of brightness.
But even at that time of day
when you see with in your space,
being bright.
That only means what's out of your space is night.
Right ?
Living in the shadows of the world.
Not wanting to be seen.
A tethered soul.
With tethered wings.
Tethering to the unseen.
Too keen not to transcend.
I got a spark, something special.
And though, dark clouds

try to cover the rays of my sun beams.
I swear to thy higher self, I'll break through.
Shedding enough brightness.
That my son's being might grasp enough light.
So he'll never walk in my shadows.
Cause he's got to glow.
Across the sky casting rainbows.
Ensuring my daughter always knows.
Even when she's old.
Long after my stories unfold.
That she's the pot of gold.
Worth more than a pot of gold.
She's got to glow.
And I'm just getting started.
That's just me flexing my chakras.
My ego saying how dare I stop ya.
My closet was once filled with dark colors.
Till I mixed it up.
Fuck it, I'm a cop some shit I've never worn before.
Starting from my core working my way up.
Discovering that green looked good on my complexion.
Matter fact, best represented my reflection.
Enlightening my projection.
Lights, camera, action.
A star is born.
A supernova.
Can't help but shine over.
Over the depths.
Making it a path.
Only finding my way back on course.

Unblinded route to source.

Distorted vision.

Contorted decisions.

Only impaired my mission.

I can remember.

Before descending to this dimension.

An agreement was made.

Past lives were paid.

I wasn't able to finish what I started, so I stayed.

In one life I was the prisoner that escaped Plato's cave.

Another life I was a runaway slave.

And now a days.

I find myself stuck in a faze.

Perhaps in a dark maze.

Discovering that the only way to flight the night,

Is to fight for my light.

I am **LIGHT**!!

My heart lacks faith in my brain, & my brain lacks faith in my heart. Neither of them can see a clear picture of the future. What lies ahead is a mystery. Even combined, they find it hard to find the answers to the questions of my life

10-9-02
2:25

Everyone fears that I am
running away from my problems.
If I really wanted to escape
I would rid my self from living
another day.
Ponder on taking my life
by falling on a knife,
Or slitting my wrist, know
long experience blissfulness.
My thoughts alone are
self capable of harm
No conscious involve no
more charm
This is the root that ~~known~~ NO
one wants to imagine
Only if they knew

I try to speak through talking
~~I try to talk through writing~~
~~But no one listens~~
But no one wants to listen
I try to talk through writing
But no one bothers to break down
comprehension
My thoughts remain alone
With no way out
Just floating in my cell
All till time patient
Will I ever be heard
Or will I be one, with no
sound from ~~within~~ this voice
within
Only my heart, my soul, my entire
~~self~~ being, takes the time to communicate
Life is full of talkers
But only few listen
I am a listener waiting to talk
My feelings are only express
Through my misconception

personality, and facial expressions
Yes I admit it is quite hard to figure
out me
Not even close to me, truly
Like the time, and that just sad
I have never like myself
Same ones with patience
Tolerance, and persistence
I was always told that you only
recieve from what you put out
I have yet to recieve
It un-fair, there are many who exist
Who just don't care
Who lives are spent constantly
working on themselves, confusing the
Karma that rotates around us
But yet they recieve all that they
wish for
My dreams and aspirations have
been constantly plundered, by
those who passion only exist
in their pockets

What are dreams; nothing
more than feelings thought
planted in your head, to give
hope; in hope to survive the
distant hopeless realm we call
life.

Life is nothing more than a last
chance; because I hope it's safe,
Dreams only exist
in minds with imagination,
fantasies that lup within
because the subconscious
is full of dull visions,
containing no aspirations.

Dreams, faith, gods, hope, wishes
and fantasies ? ? ? ? ? ?
? ? ? ? ? ? ? ? ? ? ?
? ? ? ? ? ? ? ? ? ? ?
? ? ? ? ? ? ? ? ? ? ?
? ? ? ? ? ? ? ? ? ? ? ?

10/8/02
8:39 pm

I must admit
that lately I've been dealing
with some heavy shit
Situations that no one can
see being real, because
they are to blend and
curious to see or feel.
The obstacles that I face
grow deeper than and problem
that show on the surface.
No one takes the time to
truly understand
Assumptions are made
Once again I am
face with a important decision
One that will

to me the will be a goal itself.

A— Late   October 10, 1996
      B+   3:15pm
              Neatness!

If I could go anywhere
it would be heaven. I would like to go
there because there ~~do~~ you don't
have to worry about anything. No violence
~~aggretation~~ aggravation or killing. All I wanted
peace. ~~it's~~ Heaven to me it's very peace
ful. Heaven is every positive thing you
could think of. Sometimes I think there's
not much peace for me because I set
it that way. On Earth there's to much
violence and negativity. I would want
to go to heaven so I won't have
to worry about nothing. I want
to be able to get along with everyone
I just want to chill! me too!
the Bible declares Jesus is the only way there!

Good Job   October 10, 1996 3:30pm
       to me in some

B+ → skip 2 - 3 lines
         between entries.

y'aire in middle and so are the kids your age.

The situations kids in middle school and kids my age should date. & think by the age 12 kids should be mature enough to date. Sometimes not, but i think parents should give a try. At the age 12 kids feel like they are now able to date, mainly because of their physical changes. But (mentaly) some preteen and teenagers are ready to date. Kids my age (luve) to have adult responcibilities. They want to feel like they are older. I guess dating makes you feel older huh! The only problem is too many of the kids your age are really very immature, and dating may keep them for fully developing psyically, mentally and spiritually; Not to mention what's the hurry!

October 15, 1996 9:33am
I feel like I am transforming and changing at a slow paste. But some times I feel I'm changing at a fast paste. Because sometimes I act very mature

Date - sometime in 96

Second Song

When I went to sleep
Girl I felt so weak
I didn't know what was wrong
You wouldn't tell me
We tried to talk
But now were torn apart
Girl just tell me when did all this start

Chorus- Girl just tell me
Girl I want to know I
Girl just tell me why you didn't
love me so I

Every since we've been together
I thought our love would never part
But every since we've been together you've
broke my heart

Repeat Chorus;

All I may not know what love
means.
but I know I care
And everytime you needed me I
was always there

Repeat Chorus -.

(Rap) - All I would be there for
you
And you would be there me
And I d hope you never ever leave
me
But now we're apart
You've broke my heart
And there's, nowhere to run

About the Author

Mitchell Lawrence Paschall Jr, was born and raised in Baltimore Md. Growing up in the inner city and witnessing violence and negativity, Mitchell at an early age sought out to make a difference. Through theater and working with youth both as teenager and adult, he strived to positively influence and encourage the at risk and disadvantaged. Although acting is his greatest passion, writing was later discovered to be his longest developing craft. Since the age of ten, he has been writing poetry and short stories. What started out as just something to do for school or self therapy, later would evolve into a passion and a leading source to uplift. He believes that like God, all of creation is infinite. It is one's life purpose to explore and evolve as we experience our time on Earth. Writing for Mitchell is yet another form of expression, expressing love, light and liberty.

CPSIA information can be obtained
at www.ICGtesting.com
Printed in the USA
LVHW051255271120
672645LV00007B/857